Memories for My Grandchild

A Grandmother's Keepsake Journal

welcome
BOOKS

With so much love from me

....

for you

....

on this date

....

I was born

on..

in..

My parents named me..

The first place we lived..

....

....

....

....

....

....

Some of my favorite stories about when I was a child...

....

....

....

....

....

....

....

....

....

....

....

....

....

....

....

....

....

....

....

....

....

....

> "The first cry of a newborn baby in Chicago or Zamboango, in Amsterdam or Rangoon, has the same pitch and key, each saying, 'I am! I have come through! I belong! I am a member of the Family!'"
>
> —CARL SANDBURG

The world when I was little

Things were so different then (the way we cooked, traveled, and what we spent time on)

....

....

....

....

....

....

....

Then, we didn't have..

....

....

....

....

....

....

....

Here is a favorite recipe..

....

....

....

....

....

....

Just for fun, here is what we paid for some things

a newspaper...

a quart of milk..

a gallon of gas..

The world when you were little

By the time you were born, there were some technologies we took for granted.............................
....
....
....
....

We paid so much attention to what you ate...
....
....
....
....
....

Other things that were really different...
....
....
....
....
....

The price of things
a newspaper...
a quart of milk...
a gallon of gas...

> **"**The five little puppies dug a hole under the fence…
> and went for a walk in the wide, wide, world.**"**
>
> —THE POKY LITTLE PUPPY

My mother

My mom's name was..

She was born in..

on...

I want to tell you about her family..

....

....

....

....

....

....

....

And, what I loved best about her

My funniest memory of her

She gave me some great advice that I will never forget

I am like her in some ways

And different in others

She contributed to the world in some important ways

My father

My dad's name was..

He was born in...

on...

I want to tell you about his family...

....

....

....

....

....

....

....

And, what I loved best about him

My funniest memory of him

He gave me some great advice that I will never forget

I am like him in some ways

And different in others

He contributed to the world in some important ways

My family

I grew up with..

....

....

....

....

....

Some of my best memories as a family...

....

....

....

....

....

....

My favorite trip..

....

....

....

....

....

....

Thank goodness we had pets

What I loved most about holidays

There were some beliefs that were important to my family

I will never forget

My family

My family's history

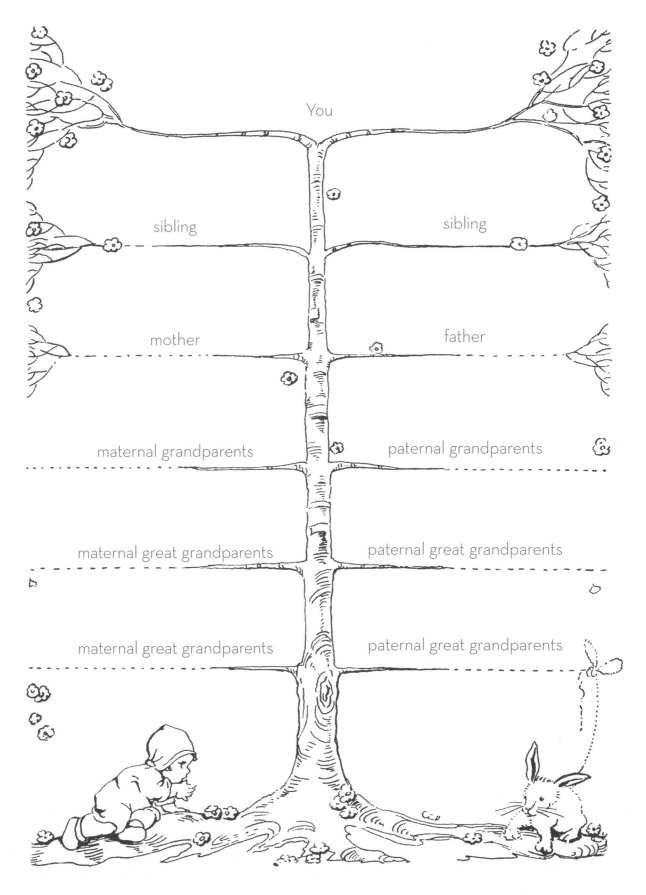

You

sibling

sibling

mother

father

maternal grandparents

paternal grandparents

maternal great grandparents

paternal great grandparents

maternal great grandparents

paternal great grandparents

My family came from ....

....

....

....

....

....

....

....

....

Some amazing people in my family are ....

....

....

....

....

....

....

....

....

....

My family

As a young child

I loved...

....

....

....

....

....

I really did not like...

....

....

....

....

....

Looking back, I had many favorites

Friends

Actors

Actresses

Books

TV shows

Songs

Singers/bands

Movies

Designers

Foods

Sports

Teachers

Subjects at school

Colors

My favorite memory from my childhood..

....

....

....

....

....

....

....

....

....

....

....

....

In some ways my childhood was so different than yours, but in other ways it was very much
the same...

....

....

....

....

....

....

....

....

....

....

....

....

When I was young

As a teenager

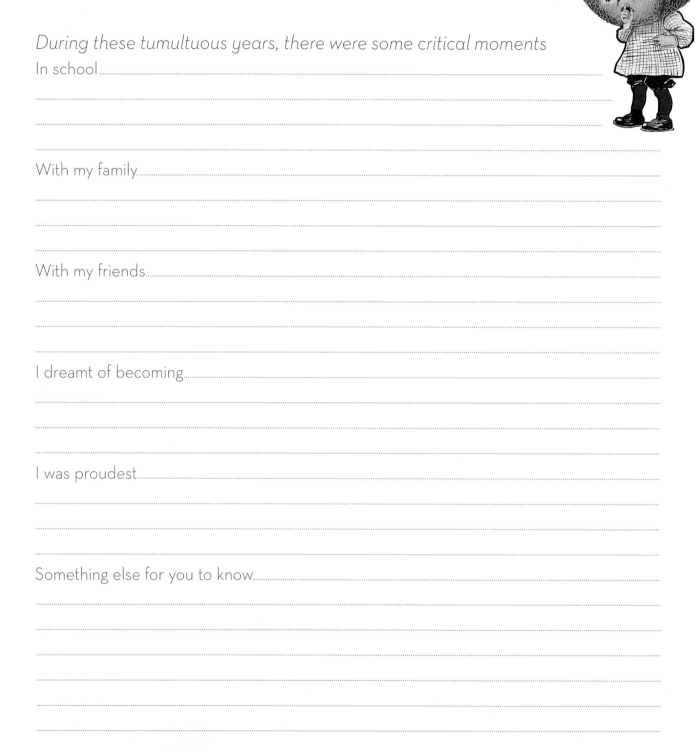

During these tumultuous years, there were some critical moments

In school...
....
....

With my family..
....
....

With my friends...
....
....

I dreamt of becoming..
....
....

I was proudest...
....
....

Something else for you to know..
....
....
....
....

" There will come a time when you believe everything is finished. That will be the beginning. **"**

—LOUIS L'AMOUR

Falling in love

I met your Grandfather...
....
....
....
....
....

His name is...
When we decided to get married, he said to me...
....
....
....
....
....

I love this about him...
....
....
....
....

This is what matters...
....
....
....
....
....

Your grandfather

There are important things to know about him

He was born on..

in...

His family came from..

....

....

....

....

....

A little something about his childhood..

....

....

....

....

....

....

Some things about his family..

....

....

....

....

....

....

....

....

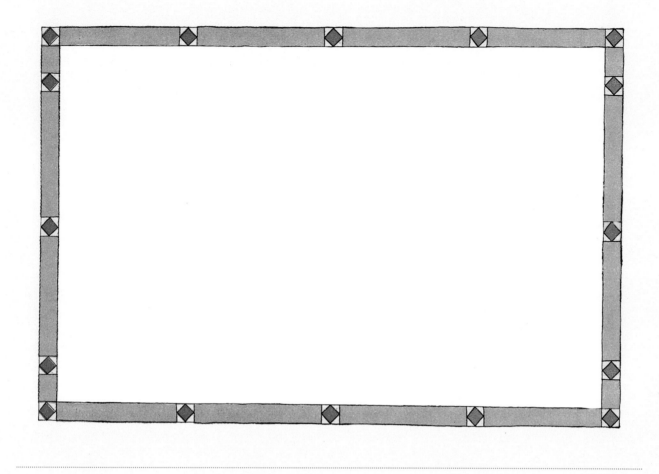

" You've got to do your own growing, no matter how tall your grandfather was. **"**

—IRISH PROVERB

Love & Marriage

When we got married I was .... years old and he was ....
What I remember most about our wedding day ....
....
....
....
....
....
....
....
....

Some of the family and friends who were there ....
....
....
....
....
....
....
....
....

I remember looking beautiful in my dress and he looked great, too ....
....
....
....
....
....
....
....
....

A few things I learned about love & marriage

"Life has taught me that love does not consist of gazing at each other but looking together in the same direction."

—ANTONIE DE SAINT EXUPÉRY

Becoming a mother

What I remember most about being pregnant with your...
....
....
....
....
....
....
....

My favorite memories as a mother...
....
....
....
....
....
....
....
....

The most important thing I ever did as a mom...
....
....
....
....
....
....

> " Making the decision to have a child—
> it's momentous. It is to decide forever to have your
> heart go walking around outside your body. "
>
> —ELIZABETH STONE

Your mom/dad

.........................was born on...
in..
The name we chose...
As a baby your..
....
....
....
....

Your.............................first walked...............................
....
....
....
....

Some of the funniest things........................ever said...

....

....

....

I'll never forget...

....

....

....

Some of........................*favorite things*

Games...

....

....

Toys...

....

....

Food...

....

....

Books...

....

....

Music...

....

....

Movies..

....

....

....also loved...

But.......................really couldn't stand..

I thought..............................would grow up to be...

As a teenager..

School was great in the following ways...

Later............................got really serious about learning...

40

I always thought your .... had these extraordinary qualities ....

....

....

....

....

....

Some of the great moments ....

....

....

....

....

....

....

But then, there were some…challenges ....

....

....

....

....

....

....

My beloved children

Names and birth dates

....

....

....

Each was different ....

....

....

....

....

....

My favorite memories about their childhoods ....

....

....

....

....

....

....

....

....

....

" People ask, 'Do you want a boy or a girl?'
The answer is 'Yes, of course.' "

—ANONYMOUS

Favorite photos & memories

Your parents

Your parents met ....

....

....

....

At first your grandfather and I thought ....

....

....

....

Their wedding day ....

....

....

....

....

When you arrived, it was a great, great day

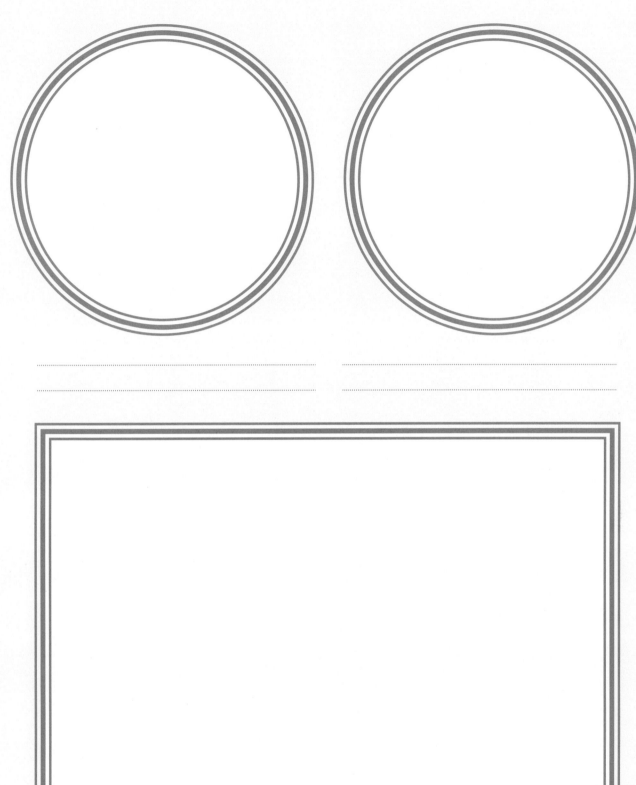

You

You were born in..
on...
at..
You weighed...
And your height..

Your name..

You were named for...

My favorite name for you...

You call me...

You said my name for the first time...

....

....

You call your grandfather..

When I first saw you I thought...

....

....

....

....

....

....

When you were one year old I took a long look again and thought...................................

....

....

....

....

....

Later, I looked again and thought..

....

....

....

....

....

You were so hilarious

Especially when you were little and

We had favorite things to do together

Oh, how you loved

But, this was definitely *not* your favorite thing

You gave me so many great things. Do you remember?

One of the best things we ever did together

As you got older, I could see you growing into the person you have become

I was so proud of you

Let me remind you of just a few of the many things I love about you

My beloved grandchildren

Names and birth dates

....

....

....

The sweetest memories I have so far with my grandchildren..

....

....

....

....

....

....

....

....

....

....

....

....

> "Nobody can do for little children what grandparents do. Grandparents sort of sprinkle stardust over the lives of little children."
>
> —ALEX HALEY

Other people in my life who love you

Holidays & special events we have shared together

Date...

Memories...

....

....

....

....

....

....

Date

Memories

59

Date

Memories

Date...

Memories..

....

....

....

....

....

....

....

....

....

....

....

....

Some of your birthdays

Date...

Memories..

....

....

....

....

....

....

....

....

Date

Memories

Other favorite photos & memories

Date ....

Memories ....

....

....

....

....

....

....

Date

Memories

You said so many amazing things

"You will never really know what kind of parent you were or if you did it right or wrong. Never. And you will worry about this and them as long as you live. But when your children have children and you watch them do what they do, you will have part of an answer.

—ROBERT FULGHUM

I have learned so much from you

About happiness

About laughter

About what matters

What I love most about being your grandmother

Some things

These are some things I want you to read, see, listen to, or do

Books..

....

....

....

....

....

....

....

....

....

....

....

....

Movies..

....

....

....

....

....

....

....

....

....

....

....

Music

Places to go

“The world is so full of a number of things,
I'm sure we should all be as happy as kings. ”

—ROBERT LOUIS STEVENSON

Some wisdom from your grandmother

Remember

The hardest thing or experience in my life and what I learned from it..

"Speak the truth, come from love, act with integrity."

—LEE HOLLOWAY

My dreams & goals for you

A letter to my grandchild

> " Become a possibilitarian. No matter how dark things seem
> to be or actually are, raise your sights and see possibilities—
> always see them, for they're always there. "
>
> —NORMAN VINCENT PEALE

_____

_____

_____

_____

_____

_____

_____

_____

_____

_____

_____

_____

_____

_____

_____

_____

_____

> **"**To laugh often and much, to win the respect of intelligent people and the affection of children; to earn the appreciation of honest critics and endure the betrayal of false friends; to appreciate beauty; to find the best in others; to leave the world a bit better, whether by a healthy child, a garden patch or a redeemed social condition; to know even one life has breathed easier because you have lived. This is to have succeeded.**"**
>
> —RALPH WALDO EMERSON

For my children's grandmother, and for my grandchild, who has given me more gifts
in one utterly magical year than I could have dreamt possible. —Lena

Published by Welcome Books®
An imprint of Rizzoli International Publications, Inc.
300 Park Avenue South
New York, NY 10010
www.rizzoliusa.com

Text by Lena Tabori
Edited by Natasha Tabori Fried
Designed by Kristen Sasamoto
www.welcomebooks.com/memories

Illustrations Credits
pages 21,26,28,40,80: E. Curtis; page 30: N. Buchanan; page 42: Margaret Evans Price

Library of Congress Cataloging-in-Publication Data on file.

ISBN: 978-1-59962-096-1

Printed in China

2015 2016 2017 2018 / 10 9 8 7 6 5 4 3

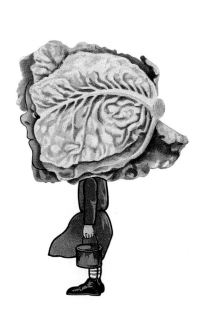